T0390407

Animal Tails

Rose Davidson

NATIONAL GEOGRAPHIC

Washington, D.C.

How to Use This Book

Reading together is fun! When older and younger readers share the experience, it opens the door to new learning. As you read together, talk about what you learn.

This side is for a parent, older sibling, or older friend. Before reading each page, take a look at the words and pictures. Talk about what you see. Point out words that might be hard for the younger reader.

This side is for the younger reader.

As you read, look for the bold words. Talk about them before you read.

At the end of each chapter, do the activity together.

Contents

Chapter 1: Why Tails?	4
Your Turn!	12
Chapter 2: Going Places	14
Your Turn!	24
Chapter 3: Tail Talk	26
Your Turn!	34
Chapter 4: Staying Safe	36
Your Turn!	46

CHAPTER 1

Why Tails?

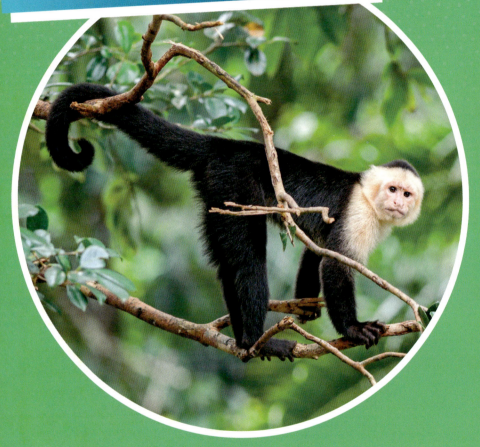

 Monkeys wrap their tails around tree branches. **Peacocks** fan their tails out. But why do animals have tails? Lots of reasons! Tails help animals move, send signals, and stay safe.

Peacocks have bright, shiny tail feathers. They mean "Look at me!"

YOU READ

Animals use their tails to find food and shelter. Their tails help them hang from branches or keep steady while climbing.

Opossums climb in trees. They wrap their tails around branches so they don't fall.

Young **opossums** hold on to branches as they move. They can even hang upside down!

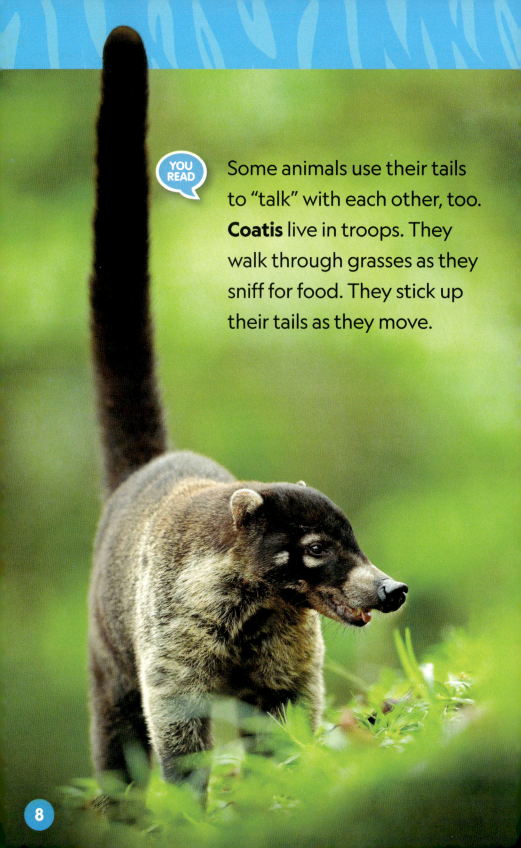

YOU READ

Some animals use their tails to "talk" with each other, too. **Coatis** live in troops. They walk through grasses as they sniff for food. They stick up their tails as they move.

 If a **coati** is lost, it looks for the tails of other coatis. They show the lost coati where to go.

Tails protect animals, too. A **pangolin** pulls its hard, scaly tail around its body. It's like a shield. It protects the pangolin from predators that want to eat it. Mother pangolins also use their tails to carry their babies.

tail

I READ The young **pangolin** rides on its mother's tail. The baby stays safe.

YOUR TURN!

Draw your favorite animal with a tail. What does the animal look like? How does it use its tail?

Going Places

YOU READ

In the spring, a mother toad hops into a **pond** to lay eggs. After a few days, the eggs hatch. Tiny young toads called tadpoles use their tails to swim around.

When they are fully grown, they won't need tails for swimming anymore.

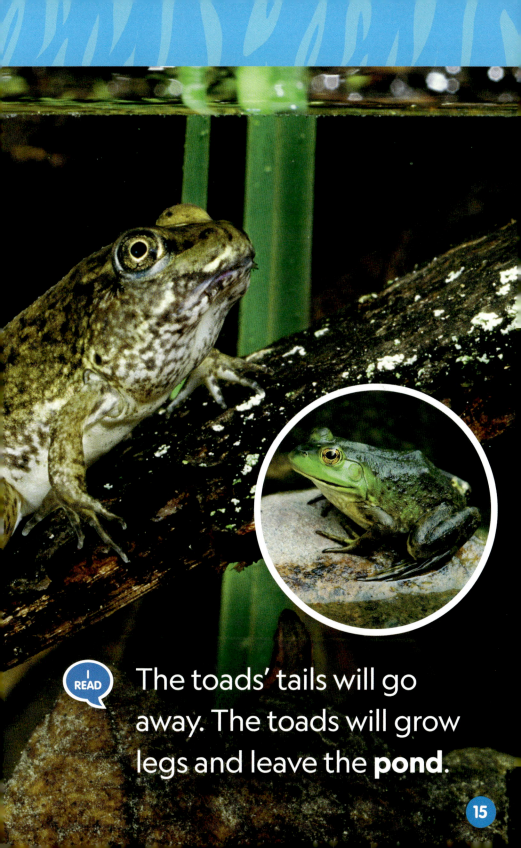

The toads' tails will go away. The toads will grow legs and leave the **pond**.

 On a warm day in the **rainforest**, a spider monkey climbs a tree with her baby. The monkey wraps her tail tightly around a branch. Then … she swings! She moves from one branch to another, using her tail like an extra hand.

I READ

The baby holds on to its mother. They move through the **rainforest** together.

 A seahorse drifts in the ocean. But when the wind blows, the water moves faster. The seahorse looks for a coral **reef** to rest in. It grabs a coral branch with its tail. Now the seahorse won't float away.

 The seahorse hides in the **reef**. It waits until the water is still again.

YOU READ

Kangaroos are famous for hopping. But did you know kangaroos walk, too?

A kangaroo bends down. It pushes its short arms and strong tail against the ground. Then the kangaroo swings its long legs forward to walk on the sunny **plains**.

I READ

The kangaroo's tail helps it walk without falling. It walks to a shady spot on the **plains** to cool down.

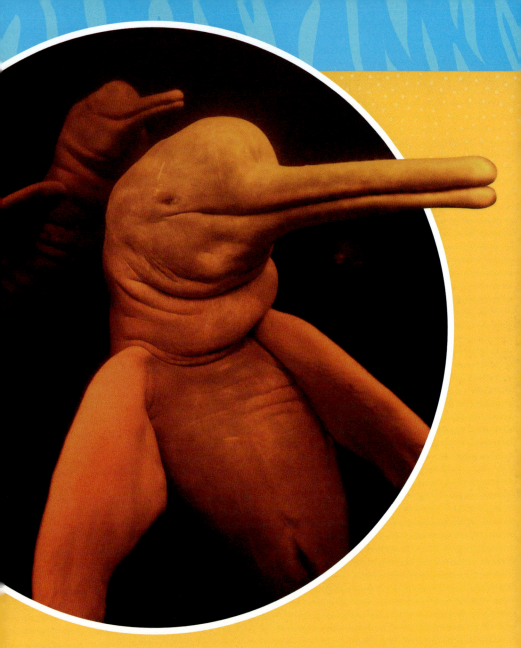

The Amazon **river** dolphin is an underwater athlete. It swims backward and upside down, weaving between plants as it goes. The dolphin's tail helps push its body through the water.

The dolphin moves its tail up and down. It swims through the **river**.

YOUR TURN!

Match the animal with the place where it lives.

1

2

3

ANSWERS: 1-A, 2-C, 3-B

25

CHAPTER 3

Tail Talk

Some animals can send messages with their tails. A tail's shape and movement can show that an animal is scared or happy. A tail can be straight or **curled**, moving or still.

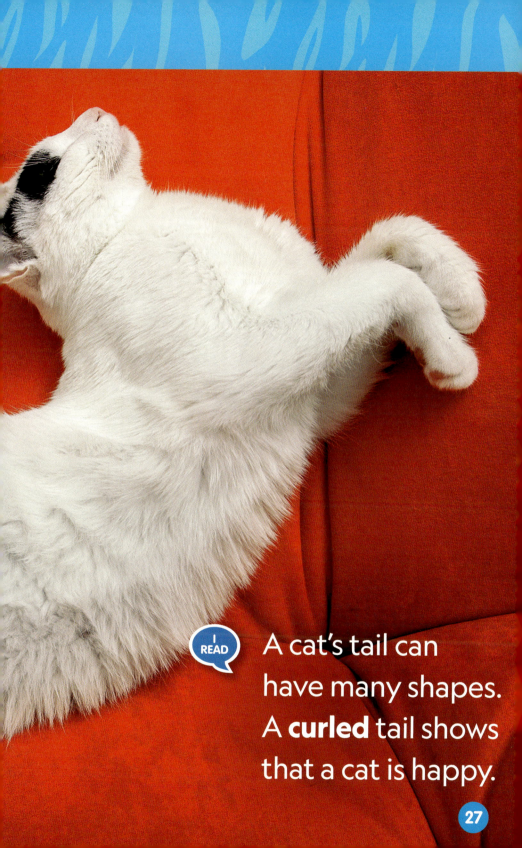

I READ A cat's tail can have many shapes. A **curled** tail shows that a cat is happy.

 Beavers smack the water with their wide, **flat** tails. If a beaver sees danger nearby, it uses its tail to alert other beavers.

 The beaver slaps its **flat** tail on the water. The other beavers hear it. They swim away.

A bird of paradise struts his **colorful** tail feathers. He is looking for a mate. He shakes his feathers as he dances around the forest.

 Another bird sees the **colorful** tail. She comes to greet to the bird.

YOU READ
Ring-tailed lemurs use their **striped** tails to fight. They rub a smelly liquid on their tails. Then they flick their tails at each other.

 Swish! A lemur flicks its **striped** tail. The lemurs start to fight.

YOUR TURN!

What word would you use to describe the tail in each photo? Use the words in the word bank below.

Word Bank

colorful
curled
flat
striped

beaver

cat

bird of paradise

ring-tailed lemur

ANSWERS: Cat: curled, Beaver: flat, Bird of paradise: colorful, Ring-tailed lemur: striped

CHAPTER 4

Staying Safe

Red pandas have soft, thick hair to **protect** them in the winter. A red panda wraps its bushy tail around its body like a scarf to keep warm.

 The red panda curls up for a nap. Its tail **protects** its body from the cold.

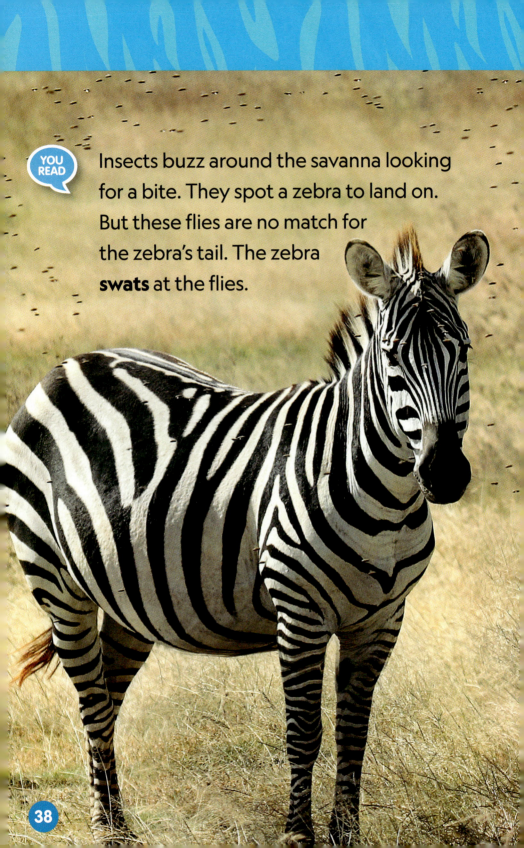

YOU READ

Insects buzz around the savanna looking for a bite. They spot a zebra to land on. But these flies are no match for the zebra's tail. The zebra **swats** at the flies.

When the zebra **swats**, the flies go away.

In the desert, scorpions are food for birds, lizards, and other animals. But a scorpion's tail can give a powerful **sting**! The tails are filled with venom.

I READ

The scorpions **sting** the animals. Now the scorpions can get away.

Alligators **store** fat in their tails from the food they eat. Their bodies use the fat for energy.

Alligators spend lots of time in the water. In the hot summer, they make holes in the ground with their tails.

The holes **store** water. The water keeps the alligators cool on a hot day.

YOU READ

Some reptiles can grow new tails. When an animal attacks a lizard, the lizard has a plan. It **sheds** its tail! The predator walks off with the tail, but the lizard walks off with its life.

44

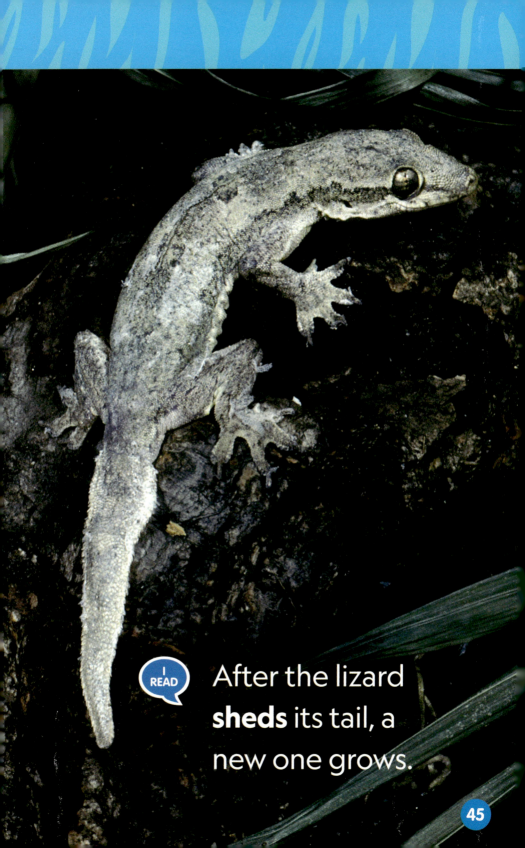

I READ After the lizard **sheds** its tail, a new one grows.

YOUR TURN!

Look at the picture. How many lemur tails do you see? Touch each tail as you count.

For Julie —R.D.

Published by National Geographic Partners, LLC, Washington, DC 20036.

Copyright © 2023 National Geographic Partners, LLC. All rights reserved. Reproduction of the whole or any part of the contents without written permission from the publisher is prohibited.

NATIONAL GEOGRAPHIC and Yellow Border Design are trademarks of the National Geographic Society, used under license.

Designed by Tom Carling and Gustavo Tello

The author and publisher gratefully acknowledge the expert content review of this book by Dr. Bill Swanson, director of animal research at the Cincinnati Zoo's Center for Conservation and Research of Endangered Wildlife, and the literacy review by Kimberly Gillow, principal, Chelsea School District, Michigan.

Library of Congress Cataloging-in-Publication Data

Names: Davidson, Rose, author.
Title: Animal tails / Rose Davidson.
Description: Washington, DC : National Geographic Kids, 2023. | Series: National geographic readers | Audience: Ages 4-6 | Audience: Grades K-1 |
Identifiers: LCCN 2019051456 (print) | LCCN 2019051457 (ebook) | ISBN 9781426338809 (trade paperback) | ISBN 9781426338816 (library binding) | ISBN 9781426338823 (ebook)
Subjects: LCSH: Tail--Juvenile literature.
Classification: LCC QL950.6 .D38 2020 (print) | LCC QL950.6 (ebook) | DDC 591.4/1--dc23
LC record available at lccn.loc.gov/2019051456
LC ebook record available at lccn.loc.gov/2019051457

Photo Credits

Cover, yakub88/Adobe Stock; 1, ultramarinfoto/Getty Images; 3, Glenn Bartley/All Canada Photos/Adobe Stock; 4, Frans Lemmens/Getty Images; 5, R. Matthew Locknane/Adobe Stock; 6-7, E.R. Degginger/Alamy Stock Photo; 8, ondrejprosicky/Adobe Stock; 9, Juan Carlos Munoz/Getty Images; 10, nwdph/Shutterstock; 11, Jiri Prochazka/Adobe Stock; 12-13 (drawing), Dolly/Shutterstock; 12-13 (crayons), Charles Brutlag/Dreamstime; 14-15, Sharon Cummings/Dembinsky Photo Associates/Alamy Stock Photo; 15 (insert), Skip Moody/Dembinsky Photo Associates/Alamy Stock Photo; 16, Adrian Hepworth/Alamy Stock Photo; 17, lunamarina/Adobe Stock; 18-19, Krzysztof Bargiel/Shutterstock; 20-21, Jurgen & Christine Sohns/Getty Images; 20 (inset), miralex/Getty Images; 22, Kevin Schafer/National Geographic Image Collection; 23, Kevin Schafer/Minden Pictures; 24 (UP LE), Hannu Viitanen/Dreamstime; 24 (UP RT), JackF/Adobe Stock; 24 (LO), kyslynskyy/Adobe Stock; 25 (UP LE), Egon Zitter/Dreamstime; 25 (UP RT), totajla/Adobe Stock; 25 (LO), scubaluna/Shutterstock; 26-27, svetkor/Shutterstock; 28-29, webmink/Getty Images; 29 (inset), Stan Tekiela/Getty Images; 30 & 31, Tim Laman/National Geographic Image Collection; 32, e'walker/Shutterstock; 33, Suzi Eszterhas/Minden Pictures; 34, svetkor/Shutterstock; 35 (UP), Robert McGouey/Alamy Stock Photo; 35 (CTR), Tim Laman/National Geographic Image Collection; 35 (LO), michaklootwijk/Adobe Stock; 36-37, AB Photography/Adobe Stock; 38, mattiaath/Adobe Stock; 39, Eric Isselée/Adobe Stock; 40-41, Mr.Suchat/Shutterstock; 41 (inset), Solvin Zankl/Nature Picture Library; 42, Images Etc/Getty Images; 43, Richard Ellis/Alamy Stock Photo; 44 & 45, R. Andrew Odum/Getty Images; 46-47, tratong/Shutterstock

Printed in the United States of America
23/WOR/1